CONSCIOUS
CAPITALISM
PRESS™

I0045591

The ABCs
of
Conscious Capitalism
for KIDs

Quick Step
FOOTWEAR

LEMONADE

CREATE A BUSINESS,
MAKE MONEY,
CHANGE THE WORLD

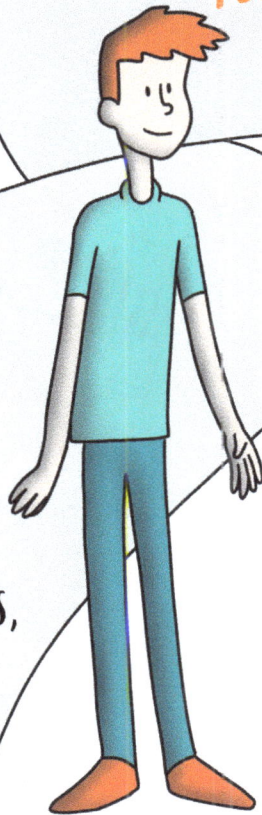

By **Laura Hall**

Illustrated by *Brent Metcalf*

Edited by *Agata Antonow*
Malary Hill

Editing **Agata Antonow, Malary Hill**
Illustration **Brent Metcalf**
Design and Layout **Sunny DiMartino**
Proofreading **Adam Lawrence, Carly Cohen**
Project Management **Keli McNeill**

CONSCIOUS CAPITALISM PRESS™

Conscious Capitalism Press
www.consciouscapitalism.org/press

rtc

Round Table Companies
Packaging, production, and distribution services
www.roundtablecompanies.com

First Edition: January 2020
10 9 8 7 6 5 4 3 2 1

Library of Congress Cataloging-in-Publication Data
The abcs of conscious capitalism for kids: create a business, make money, change the world / Laura Hall.—1st ed. p. cm.
ISBN Hardcover: 978-1-950466-11-5
ISBN Paperback: 978-1-950466-07-8
ISBN Digital: 978-1-950466-12-2
Library of Congress Control Number: 2019918805

Conscious Capitalism Press is an imprint of Conscious Capitalism, Inc.
The Conscious Capitalism Press logo is a trademark of Conscious Capitalism, Inc.

Round Table Companies and the RTC logo are trademarks of Writers of the Round Table, Inc.

To my mother, Betty Jane Hall,
who inspired me as a child . . .
and whose unconditional love inspires
me now to pay it forward.

Hey, there!

My name is Amanda and I wear many hats, probably just like you. I am an entrepreneur, a community organizer, a teacher, facilitator, mentor, and, most important to me, a mom of three amazing kids. I passionately believe that kids are powerful. President Ronald Reagan once said, "There's a flickering spark in all of us that, if lit at the right age, can light up the rest of our lives." I am living proof that is true.

I grew up learning how to run a family business alongside my grandmother, started earning my own money babysitting for families in our neighborhood when I was eleven, managed our local diner by the time I was fifteen, and the rest is history. I was also in the first class of female altar servers at my church, raised money from my classmates to save the rainforest, and was elected by peers five years my senior to run a regional youth council when I was twelve.

My pursuit of service to others and my desire to earn my own money have been intertwined my whole life. These early experiences shaped me and the way I look at the world. I was very fortunate to be surrounded by family, friends, and mentors who encouraged me and gave me room to explore. I had opportunities to go on adventures and lead from a young age, and that propelled me into a career that has provided me with nearly two decades of senior leadership in the nonprofit sector. Much of my work centers on building a culture of contribution and designing opportunities for public private partnerships. That is why, now, it is one of the greatest honors of my life to serve as the chief innovation officer at Conscious Capitalism, Inc., where I have the pleasure of supporting a global network of business leaders who are growing the purpose economy and elevating humanity through their businesses.

AMANDA

Kids have changed the world. They are changing the world. And I know that they will lead the next stage of our evolution. I want them to know that business is a powerful vehicle to do good in the world while growing and prospering in their own lives. They need to know there are thousands of amazing businesses and tens of thousands of business leaders around the world who are doing good for others while doing well financially.

I am so thrilled that Laura chose to write this book so that all girls and boys—and all of us who love them and want to see them happy and thriving—can learn about Conscious Capitalism. As a mother, I am thrilled that mothers, fathers, aunts, uncles, cousins, educators, teachers, and anyone else that has the honor of shaping young minds can now have this fantastic resource to learn alongside our next generation of leaders!

I am a firm believer that we need to provide more experiences of entrepreneurship to our children. If you are reading this now, I trust that you agree and are joining this effort—welcome! I am so pleased to see all the efforts to show my kids, your kids, and all our kids that they can be changemakers in our world while also earning a profit. We need to introduce and nurture an entrepreneurial mindset so that they can unlock the special sauce that lives inside of each and every one of them.

Thank you to every single Conscious Capitalist who is leading by example with their journey.

Thank you to every customer who has supported those businesses by purchasing their products or services.

Thank you to everyone that has told a story about their experience with that product or someone they met from that company.

Thank you to Laura for writing this book and bringing more young people into our community.

Thank you, reader, for purchasing this book—I know you will enjoy it, and please share it far and wide! You are now a part of our community, and we are so glad you are here. Reach out anytime and please let me know if you want to contribute your special sauce in some way that will bring more meaning and purpose to your life—I love meeting new people!

Let's go—our future is bright if we keep working together!

Amanda Kathryn Roman
Kitty, Antonio, and Rocco's Momma

A Note from the Author

Welcome to *The ABCs of Conscious Capitalism for KIDs*. This is a DIY (do-it-yourself) book about becoming a Conscious Capitalist. Maybe you're curious about opening your own business and are tired of adults telling you you're too young. Maybe you have an idea that your own business can do a lot more than make cash. No matter why you decided to open this book, we're thrilled. There is no better time to start a business than now.

Conscious Capitalism may sound complicated, but it's not. It's just a way to do business based on a simple idea. That idea is that when business is done the right way or consciously, it helps all people and doesn't hurt the planet.

Capitalism works. It has amazing power to change lives for good.

Some capitalists have misused their power, so sometimes people say capitalism and business is based on greed, behaving badly, and exclusion. This is just not true. Look around and you'll see lots of businesspeople in your community and in the world using their work to make the world a better place. Conscious Capitalism is changing the way we think about how to be a capitalist.

There are twenty-six letters of the alphabet, so this book includes twenty-six different ways to think about Conscious Capitalism. If you start reading something and think, "Wow, these are long complicated words," just remember that *geography* and *pepperoni pizza* are pretty long words too, and yet you've learned them. Don't let the big words stop you. Don't let anything stop you. Jump in and don't be afraid to ask questions. Don't be scared to start your own business, make lots of money, and make big changes in the world.

And don't forget to have some fun along the way. Get your friends together and get creative. Conscious Capitalism works best when you have a bunch of people working together!

Laura Hall
Peter, Paul, and Lisa's mother and
Alex, Mikayla, and Sydney's grandmother

LAURA

About the Author   *Laura Hall has spent most of her business career in the fashion industry, helping to steer famous brands like Burberry and Polo Ralph Lauren. She left her last corporate role as president of accessories for Polo Ralph Lauren to pursue her dedication for helping others and making a difference for companies building brands. She brings that passion and commitment to this writing project.*

A At the Beginning

B Business for Good

C Caring Culture

D Diversity and Inclusion

E Equality and Equity

F Free Enterprise and Free Markets

G Go Green

H Heroes and Heroines

I Impact Investors

J Joyful Jobs

K Kid Power (Kidpreneurs)

L Loving Leadership

M Money Matters

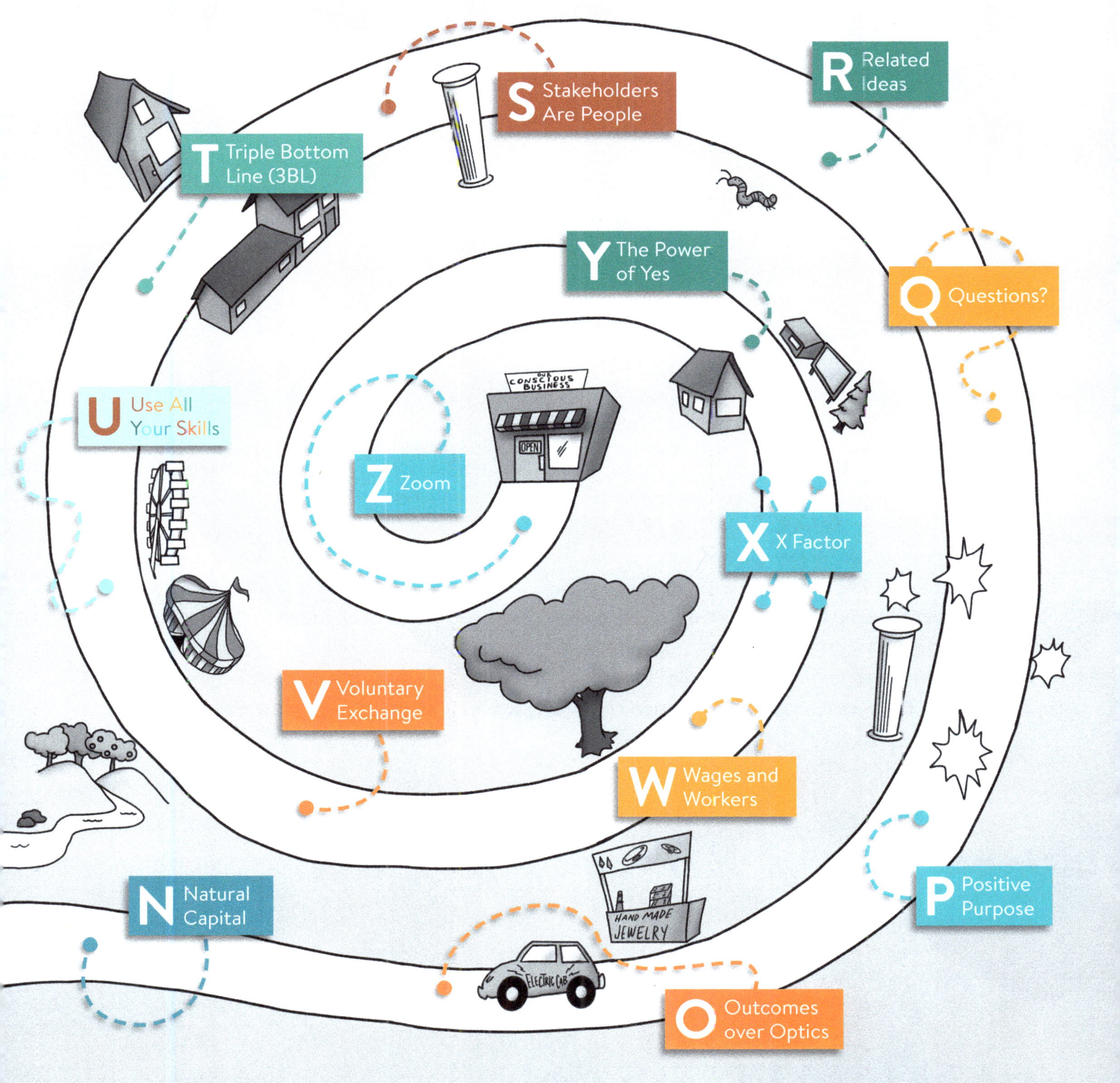

N Natural Capital
O Outcomes over Optics
P Positive Purpose
Q Questions?
R Related Ideas
S Stakeholders Are People
T Triple Bottom Line (3BL)
U Use All Your Skills
V Voluntary Exchange
W Wages and Workers
X X Factor
Y The Power of Yes
Z Zoom
OUR CONSCIOUS BUSINESS
OPEN
HAND MADE JEWELRY
ELECTRIC CAB

At the Beginning

"If you are successful, it is because somewhere, sometime someone gave you a life or an idea that started you in the right direction."
—**MELINDA GATES**, cofounder of the Bill & Melinda Gates Foundation

Capitalism.

You may have heard this word in school or around the dinner table. The word *capitalism* is used when people talk about money and business, and it's a word that has a big impact on how we live our lives.

The word *capitalism* describes a system where people work or trade in exchange for money so they can use that money to pay for things they need (like clothes and food), or things they want (like games, going to the movies, or traveling on vacation). In a capitalist society, the government does not get to decide who can sell what and how much can be charged for goods and services. Instead, private business owners are given this right, and customers get to vote with their wallets. In a capitalist society, anyone, including you, can earn money by creating a business that you love.

What is so neat about capitalism and business, though, is that beyond making money, there is so much more you can do. This is where the idea of CONSCIOUS CAPITALISM comes from. Conscious Capitalists know that businesses can do much more than make you money to buy cool things. Conscious Capitalists know that businesses can do incredible good in the world. Conscious Capitalists set up their businesses to take care of people and the planet, all while making a profit! How awesome is that?!

Because of their focus, Conscious Capitalism and capitalism look different:

CONSCIOUS LEMONADE

ORGANIC

GLASS STRAW

DISCOUNT LEMONADE

DISCOUNT LEMONADE

INVESTOR

BUY NOW! LEMONADE ONE WEEK ONLY

ℹ️ Color in light blue every part of this picture that shows traditional capitalism at work, and color in green every part of the pictures that shows Conscious Capitalism.

Business for Good

"If you're lucky enough to be somebody's employer, then you have a real moral obligation to ensure that person looks forward to getting out of bed and coming to work in the morning." —**KIP TINDELL**, cofounder and chairman of The Container Store

Have you ever seen a puppy or kitten crying for help, on TV or in real life? Did you want to help right away? You're probably a kind, good person, but did you know your brain is wired so you are that way?

A long time ago, before we had cell phones and online shows and even houses, caring for each other allowed us to survive in a really rough caveperson world. Our minds are actually set up so that when we're kind, they send out brain chemicals that make us feel great, causing us to want to be kind more and more. Isn't that cool?!

Conscious Capitalists believe that our care and compassion for one another and for the world around us can be used in business, too. They start companies because they want to do more than make money—they want to change something for the better and/or solve a problem, too.

In beginning the quest to become a Conscious Capitalist, we need to start *somewhere*, knowing that even when we make small changes, they can lead to big, world-changing results.

🛈 **If you're thinking about opening your own business, consider the ways you can use your business to help make the world a better place. Write them on the lines below.**

_____   _____

_____   _____

B

Caring Culture

"If you are a conscious leader at your company, you have a moral obligation to both create employee benefits and model the best practices that promote the health and wellbeing of your entire team."
—**MEGHAN FRENCH DUNBAR**, cofounder and CEO of Conscious Company Media

Imagine walking into a store that's as quiet as a library. You look around and notice that everyone's heads are down and they're working. There is a soothing fountain in the center, and someone walks up to you and quietly asks you whether you need help. Now, imagine walking into a store where the walls are bright blue, the staff are laughing and talking as they work, while dance music plays in the background.

It would feel pretty different, wouldn't it?

That's because these two companies have different cultures, or different ways of doing things. Culture is *how* a company does business,

and it's such an important idea that Conscious Capitalists believe it is one of the four pillars of Conscious Capitalism (flip ahead to find the other three pillars!).

Company culture is made up of lots of things. How a company treats its employees, how it makes up its brand, how it talks to customers, and its values all make up culture, which affects everything in a company. In fact, you can't have a business without a culture.

For Conscious Capitalists, culture is even more important because it helps them make a big difference for the people and the world around them. Conscious businesses work to create a culture where employees are heard and seen, and everyone involved in the company is committed to go above and beyond in helping people and the planet.

When they design a culture, Conscious Capitalists create a vibe within their company that supports their mission.

And—bonus—a conscious culture makes working for a company really exciting!

ⓘ Color in what you would add to your business culture. In the blank circles, draw what you would add yourself. Would you add in a book club? What mission statement would you have? What values?

INCLUSIVE

GREEN GET-TO-WORK OPTIONS

EMPLOYEE SUGGESTIONS

WORKER SUGGESTION BOARD

Diversity and Inclusion

"Inclusion and diversity are inextricably linked. If diversity is the thread, then inclusion is the needle." —**CFDA** (Council of Fashion Designers of America)

Take a moment to think about the neighborhood you live in or the school you go to. What do you notice about the people that surround you? Are they all the same, or do they have different experiences that help them to see the world in a different, unique way?

One of the most wonderful things about the world that we live in is that there are so many different kinds of people. And, while noticing these differences is important, it is even more important to understand, accept, and include people with different experiences and views within your company.

Conscious businesses believe that diversity and an inclusive culture make their business better. Let's take a look at what these two terms mean:

Diversity describes the differences people have in a business or in the world. This can sometimes be referred to as "the mix."

Inclusion is the act of requesting and welcoming diversity and creating an environment where all different kinds of people can grow and succeed.

ⓘ **Create as many varieties of butterflies under the umbrella as you can. Use different colors and get creative! How many different kinds of butterflies can be included in the shelter from rain?**

In other words, diversity is what you *have*, and inclusion is what you do with it.

Conscious Capitalists believe that diversity **and** inclusion are good things and that with them, your business will perform better, be a more engaging place to work, and create more profit.

It's not always easy to be diverse, however. Just because you want to hire lots of different types of people at your company, it does not mean different types of people will apply. Businesses need to work hard to become the types of companies where all kinds of people want to work. They also need to make sure they make it possible for people from different backgrounds to apply.

A diverse workplace helps people of all kinds find jobs that they love. Because of this, more customers will also want to buy from a diverse business because they see people like themselves.

D

Equality and Equity

"Fairness does not mean everyone gets the same. Fairness means everyone gets what they need." —RICK RIORDAN, American author

Have you ever said "that's not fair," especially when someone was given something that you were not? Today, I want us to think about how much we really understand the word *fair*.

Usually, when we talk about fairness, we talk about things being equal. If you get an ice cream cone as a treat, I should get one, too. But everything being equal is not always fair, either.

Let's take a look at the difference between equality and equity. *Equality* means giving everyone the same thing. *Equity* means giving everyone access to the same thing. So if everyone gets to stand at the fence to watch a baseball game, that's equality. If the fence is tall, it might make it difficult for the smaller people to see the game. But if the smaller people had a box to stand on, that would help them to see the game just like the taller people who can also see while standing on their own two feet. This is equity.

So, really, equality is only truly created by equity. If we want equality to be the end goal, then equity is the way to get there!

Conscious Capitalists believe in equity. They do everything they can to make their companies fair, so everyone has what they need to thrive.

ℹ️ **Look at the picture. The two customers at the hot dog cart have equal access to the toppings for their hot dogs, but access does not mean it is equitable. What would it take for their access to be fair? The kids on the sidewalk have equal access to the game, but it's not equitable. What do you think would make it fair? Do you think playing at a picnic table would be more equitable? Draw in your ideas on the page so everyone is able to have a nice day here.**

Free Enterprise and Free Markets

"Free enterprise has done more to lift people out of poverty than any other system. That's because people are free to say what they need and want, and other people are able to serve them to meet those needs and desires." —**ALEXANDER MCCOBIN**, CEO of Conscious Capitalism, Inc.

Don't you love the word *free*? Free ice cream. Free time at school. Free skateboards (we can dream, right?).

Well, if you live in a capitalist nation, you are free to start any business and free to charge whatever you want. Want to sell hamburgers for $1.50? Or futuristic cars for $200,000? As long as you're not hurting anyone, the government doesn't tell you what to do. This also means that you have the ability to create something that matters to you without having to jump through a million little hoops! Pretty cool, right?

Free market refers to a system where businesses get to choose what to sell and how much to charge. Free enterprise means you get to start a business without the government telling you "no."

Conscious Capitalists believe in both free markets and free enterprise. If you want to follow in their footsteps, **you're** the one who has the freedom to decide what kind of business you want to run. Your mom may tell you you have to clean your room, and your dad may tell you you can't stay out past your curfew, but the government can't tell you what kind of business to run or how to run your own company. That's a relief, right?

ⓘ **Use your freedom to sell in a free-market system! Take a look at everything on the page, and decide what you would like to charge for each item.**

F

Go Green

While we have an amazing environment around us to meet our needs, the amount of changes we can make to it without destroying it are limited. We can constantly create new things, but we can't create a new world. There is no Plan(et) B. So, it is important to use your power to keep our planet and its people safe. It means going green.

Now, being green isn't just about loving plants or the oceans or our environment. It means actually doing something to help better the world we live in. Maybe this means understanding more about how to properly dispose of your garbage, choosing to use paper or stainless steel straws instead of plastic ones. Maybe it is riding your bike instead of getting a ride in a car to go to practice. It means that you are thinking about the choices you are making and trying to do better.

Conscious businesses also want to use the power they have to reduce the negative impact on the environment. They understand that the resources we have are limited, and they are making choices to help conserve them by recycling, increasing energy efficiency, and streamlining shipping costs. They know that when they go green, customers feel that they are a caring, trustworthy business and employees can feel safe and proud working for a company that cares about our world.

Together, we all can make small changes that will improve the world around us and make it a better place to live.

ℹ **Find all the items in this picture which can go into recycling, compost, or the garbage and draw lines to the right bin to make sure they end up in the right spot.**

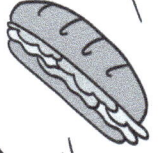

Heroes and Heroines

"My philosophy is that life is all about learning and growing, and that life can be a real adventure of learning, growing, compassion, and joyfulness."
—JOHN MACKEY, CEO of Whole Foods Market and cofounder of the Conscious Capitalism movement

Who is your favorite superhero? Now, think about what makes them so super. Is it the bright red cape that they wear with such pride? The way they talk with confidence and strength? Or is it something more?

I bet you can come up with a few specific examples of this person's strength, courageousness, or selflessness. Look behind the superhero cape and you'll probably find someone who is trying to make the world a better place.

To be a hero you need to take action, roll with changes, and accomplish your mission, at whatever cost.

🛈 **Draw a circle around each person. Give them a name and make up a story about them. What contribution can each person make? Does one person have skills in math? Is one person especially caring? Beside each character, write down their special contribution.**

There are also heroes and heroines of Conscious Capitalism. They have helped companies go green and treat communities better. They have inspired businesses to treat customers and employees with care. For example, John Mackey, a cofounder of Conscious Capitalism and CEO of Whole Foods, turned his business around, making it a force for good. He went on to cowrite *Conscious Capitalism*, the book, so others could follow in his footsteps and help change the world for the better.

Keep an eye out in the following pages to learn about the other heroes of Conscious Capitalism.

While these people are doing all they can to create courageous businesses, we also need the next generation of heroes and heroines to step up in the world of Conscious Capitalism—is that, maybe, YOU? Will you take up the torch and work to change business to bring healing to our planet and its people?

Impact Investors

"We need to start to talk about money in ways that dethrone it and make it subject to human ethics and standards of love and decency."

—JOEL SOLOMON, chairman of Renewal Funds

More money!

Did that get your attention?

In the business world, there is a special word for a person who wants to provide you with money to support your business goals: *investor.* Investors want to work with someone who they believe will make money. Businesses give money back to investors—and then some—as their business grows. It's win-win—businesses get money to succeed, and investors make a profit. Capitalism in action!

Now, there are also investors out there who care about more than the money they will make back from a successful company. Some investors also care about the positive impact that a business is having on the people and the environment that surrounds them. We call these people *impact investors*, and conscious businesses draw in these kinds of people. They believe that if doing good is good business, then investing in good is also good business.

Money to help you build a successful business AND make a positive impact on the world and the people around you? Now that sounds like a pretty good thing to me!

ⓘ **Circle or color in all the ways you can find investors or raise money for a business. Then, write down ideas of how this investment opportunity could benefit the city and its people.**

Joyful Jobs

"Life-fulfilling work is never about the money—when you feel true passion for something, you instinctively find ways to nurture it."

—EILEEN FISHER, founder of the EILEEN FISHER fashion company

I want to let you in on a little secret . . .

Someday, when you get a job, it will always involve work. It's true. *But* that work doesn't just have to be something to pay the bills. That job can mean so much more.

In fact, you can TRULY love your job, you can TRULY find meaning in your work and you can TRULY make a difference in this world.

I hope that this isn't a secret to you, but if you haven't heard this before, it is true.

It can seem far out of reach to find a job that can make you happy and make an impact, but there are many companies that make their employees one of their main priorities. These businesses—you guessed it, conscious businesses—care for the people that work for them and about the world around them, creating a pretty meaningful place to work.

Conscious bosses are honorable and caring and want to help you make a difference and contribute something good. They want you to know how much you matter, and will do what they can to help you leave a positive mark on the world!

ℹ **How are each of the jobs on this page an example of being a conscious business?**

J

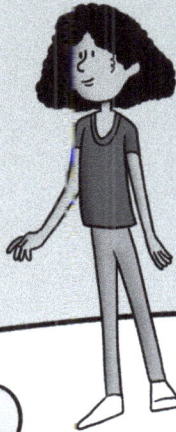

```
K D L E H B T A J S C J
R S K C U R T Y O T I D
S C N O W A U Z B H R L
I R Z E D I F L Q G W T
T J E G X L G M V I K R
Q N A P W L B N U L O A
A I R Z P E Y H P S Z M
O G M X O I Q C Y A V P
B X U R P V L X T M J O
C J F Y S R K F R T G L
N K F H I J M D M S B I
H V S U C T F L N I A N
P Y D W L E B G U R W E
D A H T E I Q C K H R S
O J B H S Z V A T C Y D
```

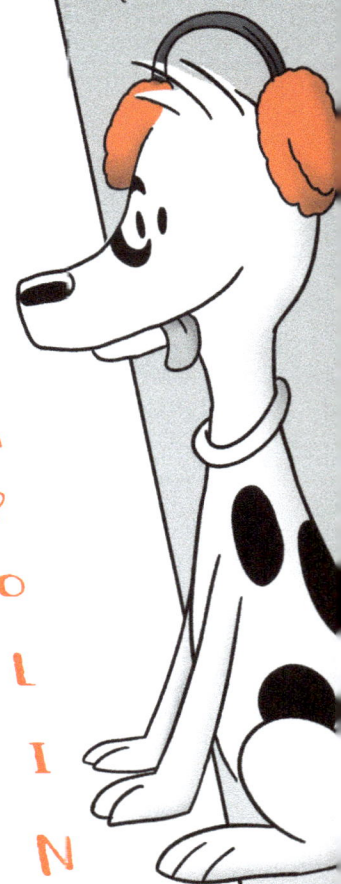

**ℹ Kids have created some of the things you use every day.
Can you find all the words that represent kidpreneur inventions?**

braille   christmas lights   earmuffs   popsicles   toy trucks   trampolines   swim flippers

Kid Power (Kidpreneurs)

"A person's a person, no matter how small." –DR. SEUSS

Don't you hate it when people tell you you'll get to do something when you're older?

"YOU'LL HAVE TO WAIT UNTIL YOU'RE SIXTEEN TO LEARN TO DRIVE."

"YOU'LL UNDERSTAND WHEN YOU'RE OLDER."

"THAT'S ONLY FOR ADULTS."

Ugh.

Well, you don't have to wait at all to become a multimillionaire and change the world. Kids of all ages have invented cool things and started their own businesses.

Kid power is amazing because, unlike adults who can often be focused only on the money-making opportunities a business can have, kids want to do something that matters, something that they care about deeply, and something that can make the lives of people around them better.

Consider Mikaila Ulmer, who became CEO of her own company, Me & the Bees Lemonade, at the ripe old age of thirteen. Not only is her lemonade sold in over five hundred stores, but she's asked to tell adults how to run their businesses. She's raking in money, still making it to math class, and her company is helping to save the bees.

Or how about Sebastian Martinez? He's the founder of Are You Kidding Socks, a company he founded when he was six. Not only is his company the place to go when you want fun, weird socks, but his business has helped organizations like Autism Speaks and others by making special socks for their campaigns.

These and many other young people are using their passions to better the world and make stacks of cash. And the truth is, you could be next!

K

Loving Leadership

"We are on the brink of an extraordinary union . . . one in which men and women alike operate from a place of authentic power. It is time for business leaders to become fully human." —NILIMA BHAT, author of *Shakti Leadership*

Love. Leadership.

We don't hear these words used together much, do we?

Usually the word *love* is reserved for our friends and family. In fact, most people in traditional capitalism believe that love does not belong anywhere in business.

But if we're passionate about our work, couldn't love be something that we include in that business?

Conscious businesses believe that business is like a person—and people need love. They know that when employees feel cared for, they gain confidence to be innovators and are willing to share their ideas and are more motivated to do their work. And you know what? Study after study is showing that conscious businesses who lead with love are super profitable and successful.

Conscious Leadership is another one of the four pillars of Conscious Capitalism. Great leaders don't always set out to be leaders, but they are on a quest to make a difference. They know that it's not about the role—it's about the goal.

These conscious leaders understand that "we" is as important as "me." They bring out the best in those around them. They know that everyone on their team matters, and they work hard to keep the business focused on its higher purpose. Conscious leaders know that creating a conscious culture of trust will create a ripple effect of love, positively impacting the profits that they make, their people, and the planet.

ℹ️ **Create your own leadership avatar!** In the circle on the leadership pillar, draw a picture of yourself. Then surround yourself with words and symbols that relate to the type of leader you want to be. Think about how you want people to feel around you, things you may say, and even things you may do as a leader.

Want more about $?

Flip to letter W!

Money Matters

"Money is like water . . . it flows. And in a conscious business, money can flow with commitment and love. Money carries our intentions. If we use it with love and purpose, then it carries those things forward."
—**LYNNE TWIST**, cofounder of Pachamama Alliance and founder of Soul of Money Institute

I'm sure you've heard the phrase "money doesn't grow on trees."

Though this is true, in business, money functions a lot like a tree—it keeps us and our business safe and protected, and it also keeps us breathing, letting us thrive and positively impact our environment.

To be successful in business, it's important to think about money as a good thing and use it to its full potential. This also means that we need to understand money and its purpose.

Conscious Capitalists believe that money, if used properly, will create opportunities for you, the people you work with, and the world that you are living in.

By allowing money to serve its purpose in a conscious way, you are not only making a profit, but you are allowing it to also serve people and the planet that we live on.

ℹ️ **Next to each dollar bill, write down what you'll need to buy for your business to improve your products, services, or culture, and then on the bill, write how much money you think you'll need to buy it.**

Natural Capital

"We need to revise our economic thinking to give full value to our natural resources. This revised economics will stabilize both the theory and the practice of free-market capitalism. It will provide business and public policy with a powerful new tool for economic development, profitability, and the promotion of the public good."

—PAUL HAWKEN, American environmentalist and author of *Project Drawdown*

Step outside and take a look around. Breathe in the fresh air, dig your toes in the dirt, listen to the bees buzzing around your head as they search for the next flower to pollinate.

These things that surround us every day are called "natural capital." The water, soil, air, and all other living things are what make human life possible, and they are also what help keep our economy flourishing.

However, there are already signs that there are fewer of these resources than ever before. Because of this, it is more important than ever to pay attention to how we affect our environment.

This is why conscious businesses do all that they can to reduce their environmental impact. They use solar panels, conserve water, and protect endangered species. They want to make sure that they are taking care of our world and working to help our natural habitats and environmental resources so they will be around for a long, long time.

Because the truth is, without them, we will lose the beauty of our environment, those things that keep us alive and well, and with it our businesses.

ℹ Natural capital is everywhere, but it's often hidden. Color in any examples of it you can find in this picture.

Outcomes over Optics

"Be in business to express yourself and serve others—not to serve yourself and use others." —RAJ SISODIA, cofounder of Conscious Capitalism, Inc.

Have you ever run out of socks and put on a dirty pair? They might look like clean socks to others, but you sure do notice the difference when you take your shoes off!

Optics and outcomes are a lot like that. *Optics* are what we can see, and *outcomes* are the actual results we get.

Businesses may not wear dirty socks, but they can look like they are doing good when, really, the true results are different.

Conscious businesses, like all businesses, have to consider both their outcomes and their optics—but they care more about getting the right and best results than looking good. They know that just having the appearance of being a good business is not enough, and they want to do and be better. They know that actions speak louder than words and that if they walk the talk, people will trust them.

So . . .

If a conscious business says they care about the environment, they might work with their supply chain to reduce their carbon footprint.

If a conscious business says they care about families, they might build a daycare in their facility so parents have a safe space where they can be close to their kids.

If a conscious business says they care about supporting their community, they might spend a day a week volunteering together as a team.

The goal for conscious businesses is to put feet to action and to speak the truth, creating a great place to work, more money and success, and a better world.

🛈 **Businesses sometimes use numbers to measure outcomes—like people served or number of animals saved—and these numbers can change the optics, or how we see business. Color in the numbers to see these businesses in a whole new way.**

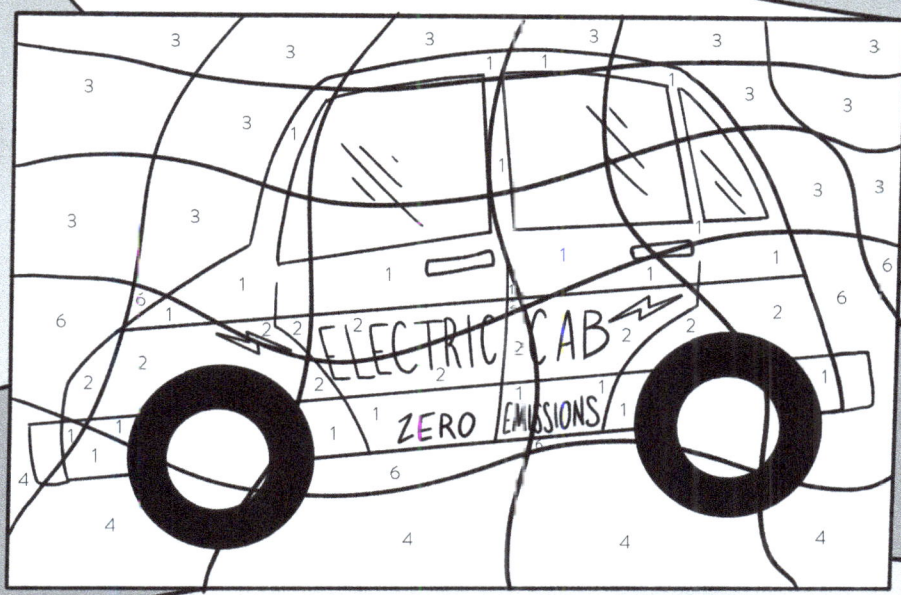

Positive Purpose

"There is no more strategic issue for a company than its ultimate purpose. For those who think business exists to make a profit, I suggest they think again. Business makes a profit to exist. Surely it must exist for some higher, nobler purpose than that."
—RAY C. ANDERSON, founder of Interface, Inc.

I want you to think about something you are really good at. Something you love to do. Something you are passionate about.

Maybe you are good at painting pictures and love to create artwork about your local neighborhood. Your purpose might be to impact your community through creativity.

Maybe you love to bake pastries and deliver them to a nearby senior care facility. Your purpose might be to sweeten the lives of the elderly.

Perhaps you have a passion for the forest preserve in your city and enjoy bringing new visitors there.

Now, I want you to think about what value this adds to your life and the lives of people around you.

When we live with positive purpose, we use the things we love, the things that we enjoy, the things that make us feel alive to help the world that we live in and the people we share that world with.

That is why Conscious Capitalists believe it is so important to understand why their businesses exist and to love what they are doing. They believe knowing the purpose of their businesses helps them to achieve their True North or their Higher Purpose.

Higher Purpose is one of the four pillars of Conscious Capitalism. Conscious Capitalists know that in order for a business to truly make a positive difference, they need to understand why they are doing what they are doing, and they need to have a team that believes in the mission of the business and believes that the profit that their company makes is only a part of the goal.

Having positive purpose is not about money—it's about understanding the why behind what you do every single day and doing what you can to make a difference with that work.

P

What do you want the purpose of your business to be? Write down some ideas in the stars, and when you have your big purpose, write it down in the biggest star.

Questions?

"He who asks a question remains a fool for five minutes. He who does not ask remains a fool forever." —CHINESE PROVERB

I, _____ GIVE MYSELF PERMISSION TO ASK QUESTIONS ALL THE TIME. SOME QUESTIONS I WANT TO ASK ARE:

ⓘ What do you wonder about? What questions about businesses do you want to ask?

_____

_____

_____

_____

_____

_____

_____

Q

How many times have you felt silly asking a question? Did you feel nervous or worry what others would think of you? Sometimes, people worry that asking questions shows they don't know something and makes them look weak.

Think again!

What if instead of being scared to ask questions, we embraced them with open arms and asked a lot of them?

With good questions, the world and business can be stronger, better, and more adventurous.

For a Conscious Capitalist, questions open doors: doors to new knowledge, doors to new ideas, doors to new opportunities. Conscious Capitalists see the heart of questioning and know that it really just means a hunger and passion for learning. They know that if you don't ask questions, you will never find out what the answer is. Successful conscious businesses do all they can to let their curiosity run wild.

So today, give yourself permission to question, be inspired to chase your curiosity, and be empowered to wonder. Because those questions just might change the world.

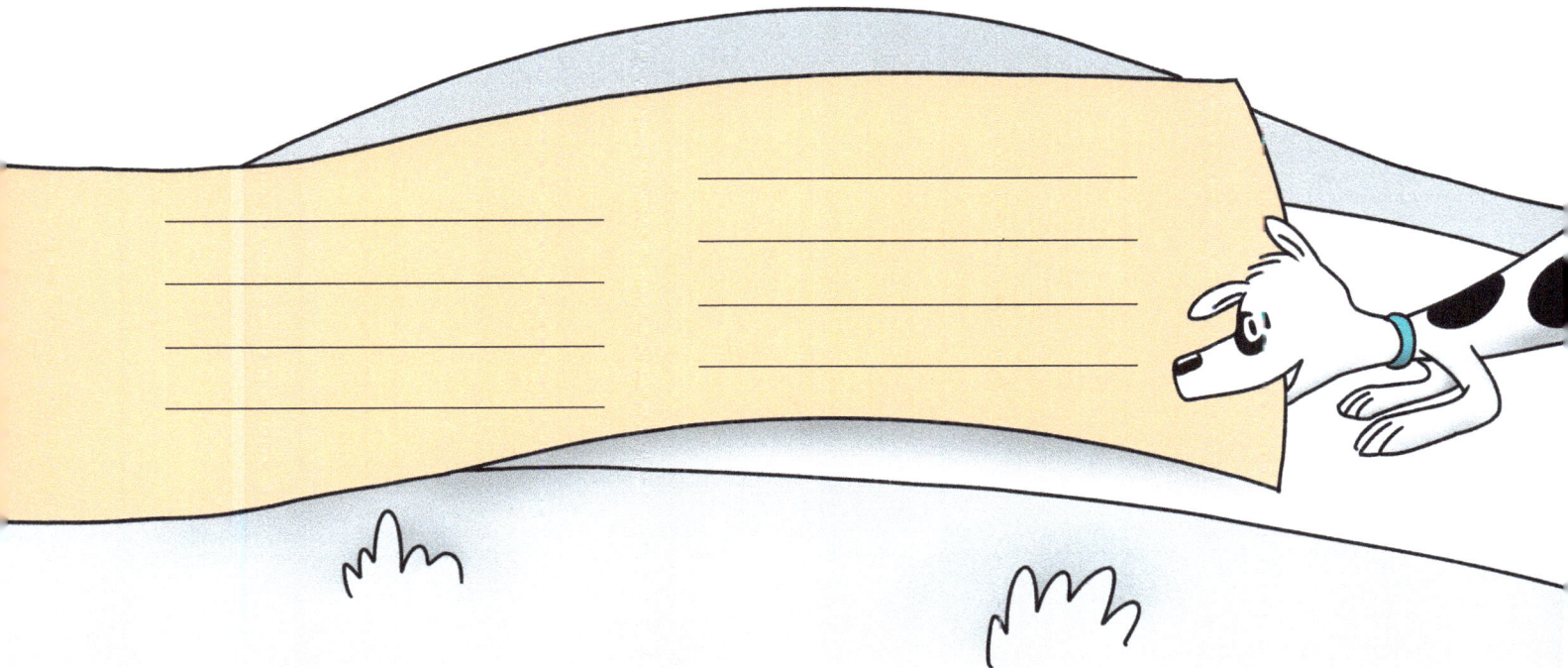

Related Ideas

Conscious Capitalism (https://www.consciouscapitalism.org/) is one way to do business differently—but it's not the only way. There are three related ways you can mix and match together to create caring companies:

"Society's most challenging problems can't be solved by government and nonprofits alone. Business has an essential role in creating the prosperous future we know our children and grandchildren deserve."

—**KIM COUPOUNAS**, global ambassador of B Lab

1

B Lab, B Corps, and Benefit Corporations. B Corporations are companies that a group called B Corps agrees are eco-friendly and committed to doing good.

https://bcorporation.net/

2

Caring economics is a way of doing business where caring for people and Mother Earth are big goals.

http://caringeconomy.org/

"The conventional view of wealth is money, possessions, and property. But the real wealth of a nation consists of the contributions of its people and nature. We need an economic system that gives visibility and value to the work of caring for people and our Mother Earth. Study after study shows that what people truly find valuable are relationships, meaning, service, and a sense of purpose. Conscious Capitalism is a way to do business that can deliver those critically needed values."

—RIANE EISLER, educator, historian, author

3

Fair trade is a way to fight poverty around the world—just by buying the stuff you would normally buy. When you see the Fair Trade Certified™ seal on your favorite products—like bananas, chocolate bars, or t-shirts—it means the people who harvested or made these things were treated well at work. That seal also means a few cents from the money you paid went into a community development fund to pay for things like new schools or medical clinics, wells for clean drinking water, housing, and other important things for the families who live and work where the products are made.

https://www.fairtrade.net/

"Fair trade is all about improving lives, but we don't do that through charity—there are no handouts in the fair trade movement. People are solving their own problems through fair trade."

—PAUL RICE, founder and CEO of Fair Trade USA

R

Stakeholders Are People

"The operation of a business is run by people. Each business has a focus to do well and be prosperous. Each person also has a desire to do well and be prosperous. This basic understanding around stakeholders (all the people involved in the business) is important in building a conscious company where everybody can win."

—MATT ALTMAN, cofounder of Sportice Apparel

A stakeholder is someone or something that is interested in or affected by a company. These could be people, the society, or the environment. When the company does well, they succeed.

Conscious businesses are careful to count everyone who is affected by a company as a stakeholder. For them, stakeholders include investors, employees, suppliers, customers, communities, and the natural environment.

Conscious Capitalists know that all stakeholders are connected; what happens to one can benefit the other. Because of this, Stakeholder Orientation—working for the good of all stakeholders—is one of the four pillars of Conscious Capitalism.

Stakeholder orientation, or integration, creates trust and cooperation between the company and those who are affected by the company. It's also a competitive advantage and makes work meaningful.

ℹ Who is going to be a stakeholder in your business? Color in all parts of this picture that show what could be affected by your business.

S

ⓘ What will the bottom line of your business be? Write down the profit you want to make, the people you want to help, and how you want to help the planet with your company.

CONTRACT

PEOPLE   PROFIT   PLANET

Triple Bottom Line (3BL)

"Capitalism has been interpreted as an exclusively profit-centric human engagement. Some have been saying to bring people and planet into the picture. This can be a good change, but it is still not fully operationalized. Are you putting people, planet, and profit at the same level?" —MOHAMMAD YUNUS, winner of the Nobel Peace Prize and founder of Grameen Bank

"Triple bottom line" is an important phrase used by Conscious Capitalists.

3BL means conscious businesses are trying to do three things at the same time. They're working to make a profit, help people, and save the planet. One of them is not more important than the other. They're at the same level.

Profit is important because it lets businesses grow and make a difference. But it's not enough for a Conscious Capitalist. A conscious business also wants to heal people, bring joy, help people, and save the planet. And instead of just giving to charity or donating to environmental causes, conscious companies help in the way they run their business. That may mean making jobs for people who need them and using less electricity in the office. Whatever they do, Conscious Capitalists are always thinking of profits, people, and planet!

"People may forget what you said. People may forget what you did. But people will never forget how you made them feel." —MAYA ANGELOU

People (Human Capital)

"Profits cannot be pursued. Profits ensue. They are the outcome." —RAJ SISODIA

Profit (Financial Capital)

"We must look at the issues around protecting our natural resources, one of the biggest entrepreneurial opportunities of our lifetime." —RICHARD BRANSON

Planet (Natural Capital)

Use All Your Skills

"Uncovering our brilliance is a process of becoming more whole and then more vibrant. We can be a crayon in other people's crayon box, or we can unleash our own full color palette on the world." —**COREY BLAKE**, founder and CEO of Round Table Companies

Conscious Capitalism is like a big box of crayons, with every crayon representing a skill or talent you have. Think about it: one of the things that makes crayons fun is that you have lots of colors to play with. When you use more skills in your business, you are more likely to create a rainbow of products and services to make your impact greater.

We want to play with all the skills that make us unique. It is through experimentation that we improve, connect new dots, and find ways to increase our impact.

Developing our skills and talents is like leaping from a box of forty-eight crayons to a box with sixty-four different colors! Now is the time to accept all the aspects of you that are terrific and to draw with all your brilliant colors.

ⓘ **What colors will you play with? Color in this page in the most creative way you know how!**

U

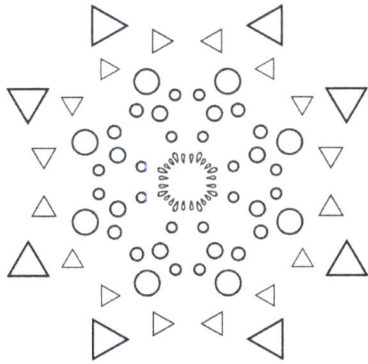

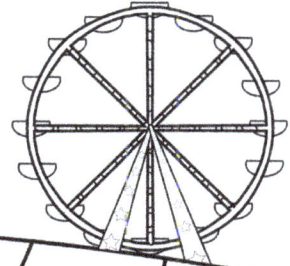

Voluntary Exchange

"The freedom to choose who you do business with is, perhaps, the greatest influence on ensuring a sense of fairness and equality in the free-market system."

—**BRIAN MOHR**, president emeritus of Conscious Capitalism Arizona

Do you remember learning about the free market? If you don't, go back and peek now.

A free-market economy is where a government allows you to run your business the way you want, without the government telling you what to do. When you talk to your customers and set up your business, though, you may not be thinking about the government. Instead, you're taking part in voluntary exchange.

RAJ SISODIA

COFOUNDER OF
CONSCIOUS
CAPITALISM, INC.

Voluntary exchange is where buyers and sellers get to buy and sell what they want. They can even refuse to sell or buy if they want. Don't want to buy a pizza at that restaurant where they don't use real cheese? You're taking part in voluntary exchange.

Voluntary exchange also means you get to go to work (or not) without someone forcing you to go to work. Sorry, though: that excuse does not work for getting out of going to school!

A free-market economy is about how the government is set up. Voluntary exchange is what occurs between your company and its stakeholders.

ℹ **You get to choose! On the sidewalk in this picture, write down all the types of businesses you could set up and all the types of products or services you could sell as part of your own conscious business.**

LOCAL HONEY

_____

_____

_____

_____

_____

_____

_____

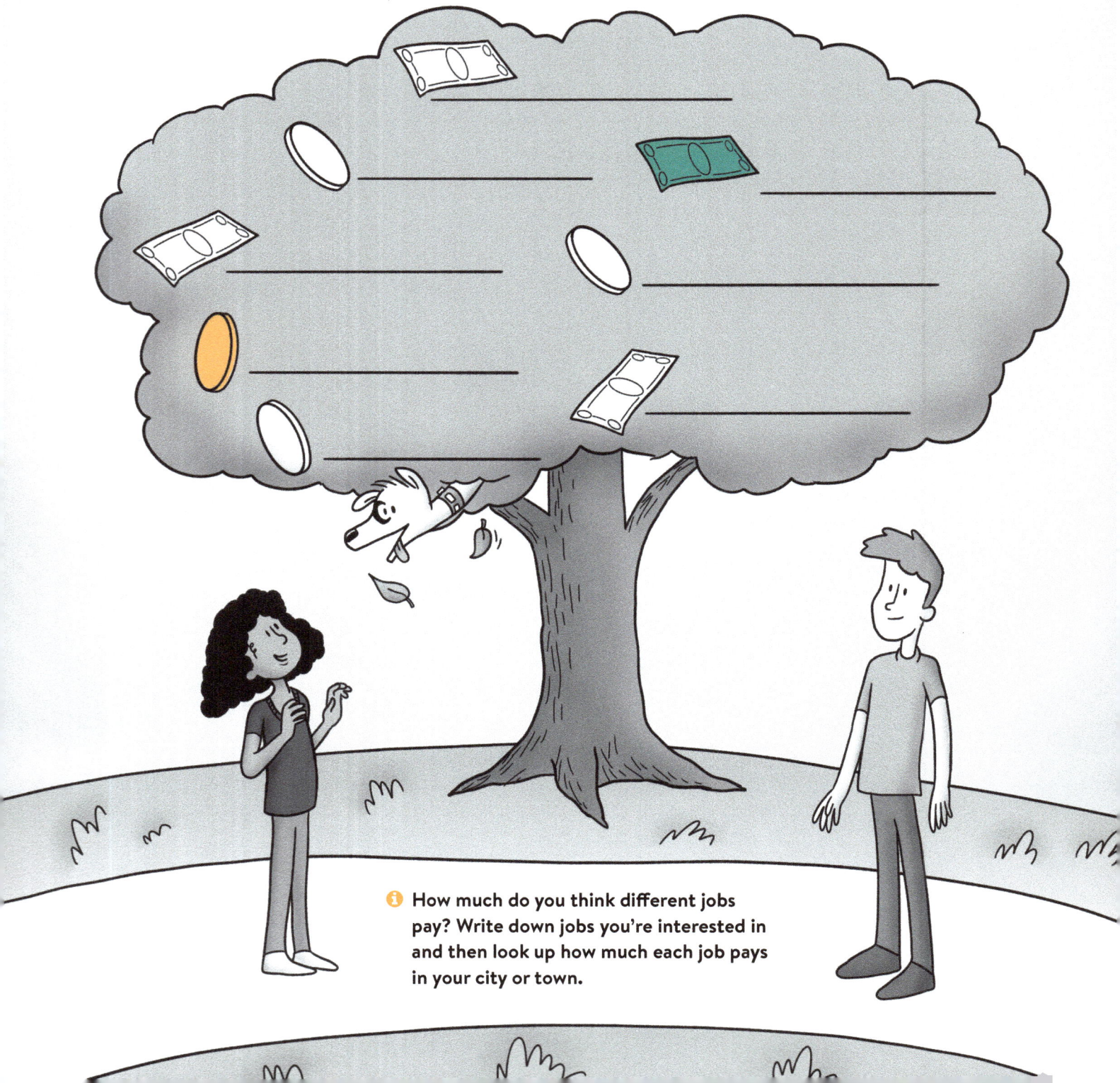

How much do you think different jobs pay? Write down jobs you're interested in and then look up how much each job pays in your city or town.

Wages and Workers

*"I don't pay good wages because I have a lot of money;
I have a lot of money because I pay good wages."*

—**ROBERT BOSCH**, German industrialist and founder of Bosch GmbH

Wages are what companies pay workers for the job they do. Conscious businesses believe in paying fair wages, but if you start talking to people about what kind of wage is "fair," you get a lot of different responses. There are three different types of wages people tend to talk about:

Minimum wage: This is the wage companies have to pay their workers. It's what the law says they have to pay, and it can be different in different states and countries. Companies can pay more, but they can't pay less.

Fair wage: A fair wage is more than minimum wage. It matches the job being done, so work that's harder or needs more school pays higher.

Living wage: A living wage is the amount of money it takes to meet basic needs (like a home and food) without needing help. A living wage can depend on where you live and how expensive stuff is to buy in that area. If you live in a big city and work in an office, you're going to need more money than someone in a small town working in the exact same type of office.

What do you think is fair for your time? Do you think getting paid $10 an hour is fair? How about $100 an hour or $3 an hour?

W

X Factor . . . Conscious Customers

"When we each make small changes in our daily lives, our efforts add up to a much larger cumulative action. You can vote every day for companies you believe in." —B LAB

An X factor is a unique or special something that changes everything. Have you ever seen a movie that was so good you watched it over and over again? Do you have a favorite song that makes you smile whenever you hear it? That song and that movie have the X factor—at least for you. There are millions of songs and movies in the world, but your favorites have the special something that makes you love them best.

What's the X factor for conscious businesses? What special ingredient makes conscious businesses shine?

Conscious Capitalists believe the secret sauce is CONSCIOUS CUSTOMERS. Without customers, there would be no business. And when customers get conscious, they share their favorite businesses with everybody and "vote" with their money by shopping at companies that align with their values. Customers have a lot of power, and when they choose conscious businesses, they help conscious businesses stay open and change the world.

So get the word out. Spread the news about conscious businesses and encourage more people to buy from these businesses. This helps Conscious Capitalists make more money so they can do more good.

ⓘ What companies have the X factor that make you want to shop there? Write down where you shop on the shopping bags. Are these businesses conscious businesses? How are you voting with your dollars?

X

RIANE EISLER

CULTURAL HISTORIAN,
EDUCATOR, AND AUTHOR OF
*The Real Wealth of Nations:
Creating a Caring
Economics*

HOW WILL YOU INSPIRE YOUR EMPLOYEES TO
SAY YES TO BEING BRAVE?

HOW WILL YOU ENCOURAGE YOUR EMPLOYEES TO
SAY YES TO DOING THE RIGHT THING?

HOW WILL YOU REWARD YOUR WORKERS
WHO GO A STEP FURTHER AND SAY YES TO
HELPING OTHERS?

The Power of YES

"The power of yes is all about the power of focus. Think about it: You get to choose how to invest your unique, abundant, wonderful energy into whatever you say yes to!" —**EMILY LONIGRO**, president and founder of LimeRed design firm

If you've been following along our adventure in this book, you may be feeling ready to say "yes" to being a Conscious Capitalist.

The word "yes" is magic in just three letters. Being able to say "yes" to new adventures and businesses lets you earn money, start new companies—even change the world. Conscious businesses use the power of "yes" in three main ways:

- **By making a "yes" culture.** Business leaders inspire their employees to be brave and say "yes" to new possibilities.

- **By building a "yes" company.** Businesses make it possible for workers and customers to say "yes" to doing the right thing.

- **By rewarding "yes" when exhibiting values.** Conscious businesses reward workers who say "yes" to living the company's values in how they serve customers and the world. Those rewards can be public recognition, a monetary bonus, a promotion, or an experience.

🛈 **Are you ready to say "yes" to the journey of being a Conscious Capitalist? As you think about the power of YES, take some time to answer the questions written on the sidewalk on the left.**

Y

ZOOM

"When in doubt, zoom out." —REGGIE WATTS, American comedian and musician

What do you feel when you fly down a hill on your bike, rush down a ski slope, run faster than anyone else, or sink the perfect basketball?

Zoom isn't about where your Conscious Capitalism journey takes you. It's about the "whoosh" your heart and body feel when you are living your vibrant life. It's the feeling we hope you experience when you open your business, make a difference, and earn your first profit.

This book is about helping you think about business differently. This final page isn't more information. It's a thank-you for finishing the book. **You are now part of the Conscious Capitalism community. Welcome! Go out there and change the world with us!**

"Money will buy you a fine dog, but only love can make it wag its tail."
—RICHARD ELLIOTT FRIEDMAN

ⓘ What would you love to do? What would help you make money and be happy? What would make you zoom out of bed in the morning? On the billboard in the picture, draw the type of life you want to live. Include all the details you want in your life.

Books, Quotes, and People

Reading words written and said by heroes and heroines of the Conscious Capitalism movement (and beyond) is a great way to get inspiration for the business you're going to build to change the world.

If you're wondering where we got the quotes from the book, in many cases we contacted people directly. We thank everyone who provided quotes for these pages! In some cases, the quotes you'll find in these pages are used by a lot of people, and it's not clear who said it first. For example, the famous poet Maya Angelou allegedly said, "People may forget what you said, but they will never forget how you made them feel," but nobody is quite sure who said it first. It's the same with the Richard Elliott Friedman words you'll see in this book. What do you think—did you want to do some sleuthing online to figure out who said it first?

We also wanted to thank all the following places where we found the quotes used in these pages:

Bornstein, David. "Beyond Profit: A Talk with Muhammad Yunus." *New York Times*, April 17, 2013. https://opinionator.blogs.nytimes.com/2013/04/17/beyond-profit-a-talk-with-muhammad-yunus/.

Bosch, Robert. "'Associates'—Not Wage Earners: Robert Bosch as an Employer." Bosch. https://www.bosch.com/stories/robert-bosch-the-employer/.

Endlich, Lisa. *Be the Change.* New York: Collins Business, 2009.

Hawken, Paul. "Capital Gains." *Mother Jones*, March/April 1997. https://www.motherjones.com/politics/1997/03/capital-gains/.

Lawrence, Kelsey. "The Most Important Takeaways from the CFDA's Diversity Report." Cools, January 7, 2019. https://cools.com/cfda-diversity-report-2019.

Leonard, Annie. "Solutions Series, Part 4: Solutions in Business." Patagonia, May 7, 2014. https://www.patagonia.com/blog/2014/05/solutions-series-part-4-solutions-in-business/.

Marcario, Rose. "100 Percent Today, 1 Percent Every Day." Patagonia, November 20, 2016. https://www.patagonia.com/blog/2016/11/100-percent-today-1-percent-every-day/.

"Richard Branson on Climate Change: 'If We Don't Change, Mother Nature Will Force Us To.'" *National Geographic*, November 7, 2011. https://blog.nationalgeographic.org/2011/11/07/richard-branson-on-climate-change-if-we-dont-change-mother-nature-will-force-us-to/.

Riordan, Rick. *The Red Pyramid.* New York: Disney Hyperion Books, 2010.

Dr. Seuss. *Horton Hears a Who!* New York: Random House, 1982.

Solomon, Joel. "Money as a Love Story." Interview by Debra Joy. Debra Joy. https://debrajoy.me/tag/joel-solomon.

Watts, Reggie. "Reggie Watts." Interview by Tina Essmaker. The Great Discontent, December 6, 2016. https://thegreatdiscontent.com/interview/reggie-watts.

ELEVATE HUMANITY
THROUGH BUSINESS.

Conscious Capitalism, Inc., supports a global community of business leaders dedicated to elevating humanity through business via their demonstration of purpose beyond profit, the cultivation of conscious leadership and culture throughout their entire ecosystem, and their focus on long-termism by prioritizing stakeholder orientation instead of shareholder primacy. We provide mid-market executives with innovative learning exchanges, transformational storytelling training, and inspiring conference experiences all designed to level-up their business operations and collectively demonstrate capitalism as a powerful force for good when practiced consciously.

We invite you, either as an individual or as a business, to join us and contribute your voice. Learn more about the global movement at www.consciouscapitalism.org.

CONSCIOUS CAPITALISM®